W9-BLH-542

2008

Ferris Wheel!

The Texas Star in Dallas, Texas, is the largest Ferris wheel in the Western Hemisphere. It is 212 feet tall.

George Ferris and His Amazing Invention

Dani Sneed

Enslow Elementary

an imprint of

Enslow Publishers, Inc.

40 Industrial Road
Box 398
Berkeley Heights, NJ 07922
USA

http://www.enslow.com

Content Advisers

James G. Ferris
Great-Great Nephew of
George Washington Gale Ferris, Jr.

Norman D. Anderson
Professor Emeritus of Science Education,
North Carolina State University
Author of *Ferris Wheels: An Illustrated History*

Series Literacy Consultant

Allan A. De Fina, Ph.D.
Past President of the New Jersey Reading Association
Chairperson, Department of Literacy Education
New Jersey City University

Library of Congress Cataloging-in-Publication Data

Sneed, Dani.
　　Ferris wheel! : George Ferris and his amazing invention / by Dani Sneed.
　　　　p. cm. — (Genius at work! : great inventor biographies)
　　Includes bibliographical references and index.
　　ISBN-13: 978-0-7660-2834-0
　　ISBN-10: 0-7660-2834-8
　　1. Ferris, George Washington Gale, 1859–1896—Juvenile literature. 2. Civil engineers—United States—
　　　　Biography—Juvenile literature. 3. Ferris wheels—History—Juvenile literature. I. Title.
　　TA140.F455S64 2008
　　624.092—dc22
　　[B]
　　　　　　　　　　　　　　　　　　　　　　　　　　　　2007010605

Printed in the United States of America

10 9 8 7 6 5 4 3 2 1

To Our Readers:
We have done our best to make sure all Internet Addresses in this book were active and appropriate when we went to press. However, the author and the publisher have no control over and assume no liability for the material available on those Internet sites or on other Web sites they may link to. Any comments or suggestions can be sent by e-mail to comments@enslow.com or to the address on the back cover.

Photo Credits: Artville, p. 6; Brandon Marshall, p. 1 (top left); Chicago History Museum, pp. 1 (bottom right, ICHi-10257), 3 (bottom inset, ICHi-10257), 3 (background, ICHi-02440), 11 (ICHi-10257), 18 (ICHi-02436), 21 (ICHi-02440), 24 (ICHi-21713), 25 (ICHi-00018), 26 (ICHi-00027), 27 (ICHi-17398); Harper's Weekly, August 5, 1893, p. 22; © 2007 Jupiterimages Corporation, pp. 5, 13, 28; Library of Congress, pp. 4, 8, 14; Paul V. Galvin Library-Illinois Institute of Technology, p. 19; Photographic Collection, Institute Archives and Special Collections, Rensselaer Polytechnic Institute, Troy, NY, pp. 9 (AC20), 12; Scientific American, July 1, 1893, pp. 17, 20; Shutterstock, p. 7; Smithsonian Institution Libraries, Hubert Howe Bancroft, p. 23; Tom Hoffman, p. 3 (top inset).

Front Cover Photos: Chicago History Museum (inset, ICHi-10257); Kumao (background).

Back Cover Photo: © Julien Hery.

Contents

Grover Cleveland was president of the United States
when the 1893 World's Fair opened in Chicago, Illinois.

Chapter 1

A Dreamer Is Born

Chicago was chosen to have the 1893 World's Fair. The fair's planners wanted to impress the crowds that were sure to attend. Just four years earlier, the 984-foot Eiffel Tower had been built for the Paris World's Fair. The tower was like an iron bridge to the sky. American civil engineers competed in a nationwide contest for an idea to outdo the French Eiffel Tower.

The boldest ideas were for taller towers. Then one engineer had a different

More than two hundred million people have visited the Eiffel Tower since it was completed in 1889.

idea. George Ferris drew plans for a 250-foot wheel that could carry over two thousand people high into the sky. It seemed like a fantasy. Could George design and build such a wheel?

George Washington Gale Ferris, Jr. was born on February 14, 1859, on a farm in Galesburg, Illinois. Martha Ferris, his mother, named him after his father. He was their ninth child.

Five years later George's family sold their dairy farm to move west. They crossed the country in several covered wagons to a ranch near Carson City, Nevada. Young George loved horses, lassos, and boots with spurs. He thought ranching was the best job a person could have.

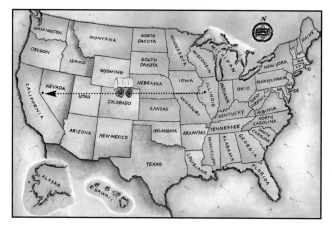

In 1864, George's family moved west from Galesburg, Illinois, to Carson City, Nevada.

Near George's home on the Carson River, a huge waterwheel slowly turned in the river. The wheel lifted buckets of water and dumped the water into a tank. Horses and cattle drank the cool water from the tank. George watched the huge wheel with delight. Legend has it that he dreamed of riding on the waterwheel.

Some people think George got his idea by watching a water wheel near his home.

As a teen George went to the California Military Academy in Oakland, California. He then continued his education at Rensselaer Polytechnic Institute (RPI) in Troy, New York.

George enjoyed attending RPI. He was voted class president, sang in the glee club, joined the rifle club, and played on the baseball team. His oldest sister, Margaret, helped by sending him money. He wrote to her saying that he was

George Ferris grew up near Carson City, Nevada.

George's Ninth Street Bridge crossed the Allegheny River in Pittsburgh, Pennsylvania.

"anxious to finish" his schooling. He promised to pay back the money.

George graduated from RPI as a civil engineer in 1881. He had several jobs planning and building train tracks, tunnels, and bridges. Two of the bridges he was in charge of building were made with an amazingly strong new metal—steel. Soon George became a steel expert.

A Wheel Idea

For George, 1886 was a big year. He married Margaret Ann Beatty from Canton, Ohio. He also started his own steel business, G.W.G. Ferris & Company, in Pittsburgh, Pennsylvania.

By 1890, Chicago buzzed with excitement as it planned the World's Fair. A year before at the Paris World's Fair, all were astonished by the Eiffel Tower. The construction chief of the Chicago fair, Daniel Burnham, started a contest for an idea to outdo the tower.

George traveled to Chicago. He heard Burnham speak about the contest to civil engineers. They all wanted to build taller towers. Mr. Burnham asked, "What's wrong with you engineers? Towers of various kinds have been proposed, but towers are not original." George decided to build something different.

While eating dinner with other engineers in Chicago, George said he "hit upon the idea." He began drawing what he called a "monster wheel." He decided on details like the size of the wheel and the cost of a ticket. George, a bridge builder, was basically planning a big round tension bridge.

George knew how to build bridges. He thought of his wheel as a big round bridge.

His friends at the table all said that a 250-foot-tall monster wheel would never work. They thought a wheel that big would break under its own weight.

George did not give up. He showed his idea to his friend William Gronau. The monster wheel would be a tension wheel with spokes like a bicycle. George wanted to be sure the wheel would not crumple in rain, wind, or ice. Gronau checked if the wheel would be safe when loaded with the weight of more than two thousand riders. The math showed it would work.

William Gronau, George's friend, also went to RPI.

George took his plans to Daniel Burnham. George was determined. His idea was not a taller tower. George's plan for a giant wheel people could ride on was original.

Burnham shook his head. "Your wheel is so flimsy it would collapse, and even if it didn't, the public would be afraid to ride in it," the fair's construction chief said.

George started to roll up his drawings. "You are an architect, sir, I am an engineer, and my wheel represents strictly an engineering problem. The spokes may seem flimsy, but they are more than strong enough." He tucked his drawings under his arm, then softly added, "I feel that no man should prejudge another man's idea unless he knows what he's talking about."

13

Tension Wheels

George Ferris's big wheel can be compared to a bicycle wheel. Both are tension wheels. In a tension wheel, the wheel and its load are supported by spokes. As the wheel turns, the spokes share the weight of the load.

Bicycle spokes are made of strong steel wire. They work together to support the weight of the rider as the wheels turn.

Daniel Burnham was a famous architect. He created building plans for parts of many cities.

"Let me have your drawings, Mr. Ferris," Burnham said, smiling. He gave them to the World's Fair directors to look at. But the directors decided against a wheel for the fair. They were sure it could not survive Lake Michigan's strong winds. People started calling George's plan "G.W.'s cockeyed dream."

George's wheel was still a dream. But as an engineer, he knew how to design and build ideas from a dream. He would make his wheel real.

Chapter 3

Racing to Build the Wheel

In November 1892, the World's Fair directors still had nothing to beat the Eiffel Tower. They finally agreed to let George build his wheel. But he would have to pay for the wheel himself and get it done in time for the fair's opening on May 1, 1893.

George needed $400,000. He asked bank after bank to lend him money to build a 250-foot wheel. He was laughed back into the street.

Even without the money, George boldly ordered the parts he needed. Next, with the help of friends, George found some wealthy investors for the wheel. The investors said the wheel should be called the Ferris Wheel and not the Monster Wheel. George agreed.

In January, George hired a crew to dig eight holes at the fair for the concrete base. The wheel full of riders would weigh more than 2 million pounds. A very solid base was needed to hold all this weight. The crew chopped the frozen ground, and then dug through sand. They finally hit rock thirty-five feet down.

As the concrete was poured into the cold ground, it froze before it hardened. There was no time to wait for warmer weather. The fair would open soon. What could George do? He piped steam into the concrete. Finally, the concrete hardened.

Five freight trains chugged into the construction site carrying the parts needed to build the wheel. Two towers were built to hold it. Cranes lifted the axle up to the top of the towers and settled it between them. At the time, the axle was the largest piece of steel ever made in the United States.

To the clanking of tools and squeaking of bolts, the first section of the wheel was hung by its spokes. Then each section, shaped like a piece of pie, was added. Soon it was time for the last section. Would it fit perfectly? To George's relief, it did.

The axle of the first Ferris Wheel weighed about fifty tons. Here workers posed for a picture as they prepared to lift it 140 feet to the tops of the towers.

Two powerful engines were placed under the wooden platform that was built for riders to get onto the wheel. Only one engine was needed to turn the wheel. George put in two in case one engine broke. The backup engine could turn the wheel and bring people safely back down.

By this time, the fair had already opened, and the wheel was not finished. George knew just one mistake could mean disaster, but he was determined to keep going. As soon as the wheel was hung, George told the workers to "turn the wheel or tear it off at the towers." Several brave workers took a free first ride, clinging to the

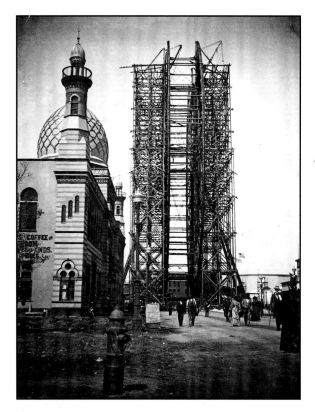

The Ferris Wheel was built inside a giant framework, seen here.

wheel as it began to move. People strolling among the exhibits stopped and watched in awe as the huge wheel spun around with workers dangling off.

George's friend William Gronau watched the wheel's first turn. Gronau sent a message to George, saying, "I could have yelled aloud for joy!" George's experiment worked. The wheel turned trouble free. The people who called his plan cockeyed were wrong. George told the crew to work day and night to hang the carriages.

On June 10, the crew began hanging the thirty-six carriages. Each wooden carriage could hold sixty people and had five glass windows on each side. Iron grills

edge of wheel

chain

The engine turned the wheel with a huge chain.

19

Workers began hanging the carriages only a few days before the Ferris Wheel officially opened.

covered the windows because George did not want someone to fall out.

With the wheel not quite finished, George boldly mailed 2,000 cards to family and friends. The cards were invitations for a free ride on the wheel's opening day.

Still, there were many people who thought the wheel was unsafe. Newspaper reporters compared the spokes to a spider's web. Would anyone dare to ride the Ferris Wheel?

Chapter 4

Queen of the Midway

At three o'clock on June 21, 1893, a big brass band played "America" from a carriage high on the wheel. Flags flew. Banners of stars and stripes hung from each carriage. A crowd gathered.

George gave a speech from the platform. He thanked his wife, Margaret, for encouraging him. As the crowd cheered, Margaret handed him a golden whistle. George blew loudly to signal the first ride. Men in blue coats and white pants opened the doors to the

The Ferris Wheel opened for business on June 21, 1893. It was 250 feet across.

six lowest carriages. George, Margaret, and the mayor of Chicago joined the excited guests to enjoy the ride.

Filled to the limit, the wheel could hold 2,160 people at a time. After taking twenty minutes to spin around once, the wheel stopped and the conductor called, "All out."

Not only did people dare to ride the Ferris Wheel, they waited in line to do so. Couples were

Iron bars on the windows prevented riders from falling out of the carriages.

A ride on the Ferris Wheel cost fifty cents, which was also how much it cost to get into the fair.

begging to be married at the top. George said no, but offered them his office instead. The wheel was soon called "Queen of the Midway."

Two quarters could buy someone ten rides on the carousel, but only one ride on the Ferris Wheel. The high price didn't keep children or adults off the wheel. From eight o'clock in the morning until eleven o'clock at night, people came to ride. To make nighttime rides magical, George outlined the wheel with another new invention—light bulbs.

The fair closed on October 30, 1893. Soon the wheel stopped spinning for the winter.

About 1.5 million people rode the Ferris Wheel at the fair.

Chapter 5

The Wheel Stops Turning

In the spring of 1894 George hired a crew to take down the wheel. It took them three months to unbolt the pieces, number each of them, and load them onto a train's flatcars. The wheel spent the rest of that year on a railroad track in Chicago.

This photo shows the wheel being set up on North Clark Street in Chicago.

George considered what to do with his wheel. Coney Island, New York, and even London wanted the wheel. But in early 1895, George decided to set the wheel spinning again in a Chicago park on North Clark Street. Stoves were added to each

25

carriage for cozy winter rides. Even so, there were too few riders. The Ferris Wheel was costing more to run than it earned in ticket sales. George finally ran out of money and had to sell his wheel. The Chicago House Wrecking Company paid $8,150 for the wheel.

Not enough people came to ride the Ferris Wheel on North Clark Street. It was costing too much to run.

Things were taking a bad turn for George. He owed money. After a disagreement, his wife, Margaret, went home to live with her family in Ohio. Then in late November 1896, George Ferris became very ill. He checked into Mercy Hospital in Pittsburgh. Five days later, on November 22, 1896, George died. History doesn't reveal exactly what sickness George died from, but overwork and wheel worries had probably hurt his health.

George's Ferris Wheel enjoyed one last fling. The Chicago House Wrecking Company had not sold the metal as scrap. Instead they moved the Ferris Wheel to St. Louis, Missouri, for the 1904 World's Fair. It was again enjoyed by many. But when the fair closed, some people in St. Louis complained that the Ferris Wheel was ugly. They wanted it removed. No other large fairs were being planned at that time. On May 11, 1906, a hundred pounds of dynamite were exploded under the foundation of George's wheel. Then the steel was sold for scrap metal.

After the World's Fair in St. Louis, the Ferris Wheel was scrapped.

Today, the London Eye in London, England, is one of the world's most famous Ferris wheels. About ten thousand people ride it each day.

No tombstone, patent, or fortune bears George Ferris's name. But don't feel sorry for him. Even though his original Ferris Wheel is no more, his name and idea remain famous. Because George dared to dream big and follow his dream, today millions of people all over the world have a great time riding Ferris wheels.

1859   Born on February 14 on a farm in Galesburg, Illinois.

1864   Moves to a ranch near Carson City, Nevada.

1876   Graduates from the California Military Academy.

1881   Earns a degree in civil engineering from Rensselaer Polytechnic Institute.

1886   Starts steel business, G.W.G. Ferris & Company. Marries Margaret Ann Beatty.

1890   Attends Chicago World's Fair engineering meeting and is inspired to design something original to outdo the Eiffel Tower. Draws his concept of the Ferris Wheel.

1893   Begins overseeing construction of the Ferris Wheel in January. Opens the Ferris Wheel to the Chicago World's Fair in June. Fair closes in October.

1895   Ferris Wheel turns again on North Clark Street in Chicago.

1896   Dies on November 22 in Pittsburgh, Pennsylvania.

1904   Ferris Wheel set up for the last time at the St. Louis World's Fair.

1906   Ferris Wheel is destroyed on May 11.

architect—Someone who creates plans for buildings.

axle—The rod in the center of a wheel.

civil engineer—Someone who is trained to draw and build structures like bridges and roads.

concrete—A mixture of sand, gravel, cement, and water used to build sidewalks, bases of buildings, and more.

investor—A person who gives money for something, like starting a company, believing they will get back more money in the future.

midway—An area of a fairground where rides, shows, and games are located.

patent—A legal paper that gives only the inventor the right to make and sell his or her invention.

polytechnic institute—A school that teaches industrial arts and applied sciences like engineering. "Poly" means many, and "technic" means arts.

spoke—A thin rod or wire connecting a wheel to its axle.

steel—A strong, hard metal made of iron, carbon, and other materials.

tension—The tightness of a rope or wire.

Books

Alter, Judy. *Amusement Parks: Roller Coasters, Ferris Wheels, and Cotton Candy.* Danbury, Conn.: Scholastic Library Publishing, 1997.

Kassinger, Ruth. *Iron and Steel: From Thor's Hammer to the Space Shuttle.* Minneapolis: Twenty-First Century Books, 2003.

Smith, A.G. *Cut and Assemble a Ferris Wheel.* Mineola, N.Y.: Dover Publications, Inc., 1992.

St. George, Judith. *So You Want to Be an Inventor?* New York: Penguin, 2005.

Internet Addresses

Amusement Park Rides and Their Inventors
http://kids.patentcafe.com/inventors/circus.asp

Internet Fairground History: Ferris Wheel Research
http://library.thinkquest.org/C002926/history/ferris1.html